Lemon Cake ©

All ri

Presentation by *BookLeaf Publishing*

Web: www.bookleafpub.com

E-mail: info@bookleafpub.com

ISBN: 9789357441575

First edition 2023

DEDICATION

To My Grandad

For fostering my love of reading, and always questioning Black Holes.

Lemons

The pain was oh so bitter, but the reality so sweet
For in the torment open doors, a new version she did meet
Of broken edges, tear streaked cheeks and battle scars
pronounced
But strength turn to resilience and a brand new 'her'
announced.
Within the change of time to see, a proud empowered force
And the ability to focus and not be thrown off course.
The writing gave her purpose and a legacy to leave
Although the bonus of it all was that her life she did retrieve.

Mixing

Stare at me but really look
Beneath the pages of my book
Dig deep to find the heart within
Flick through the chapters then begin
To understand the path I have wandered
Mistakes, lessons, stumbled, blundered
Standing out, not fitting in
Every gain and every sin
Read without judgement and soon you will see
A very tiny part of me.

Zest

The lights were blinding, the songs were loud
He felt suffocated, in the crowd
No place to hide, nor toy to clutch
He couldn't articulate 'this is all too much'
And when all the people did come near
His bright blue eyes released a tear
Which opened up his padlocked brain
To being different once again
The flapping arms, the hands on ears
The comments, chuckles, looks and sneers
So quickly lost but still so proud
The lights were blinding, the songs were loud.

Time

Tears fall from her eyes
As she relives the pain
Knowing that her view of the world
Will never feel the same

Button pushed and opened doors
Trying to process the feelings
Reassurance and guaruntees
That the offload will lead to healing

No matter what she speaks about
The obstruction in her trachea felt real
A jungle in her stomach
A stampede, an attempt to conceal

Pushing out all the troubled emotion
Did feel like a release
The anxiety and big black cloud
Would eventually decrease

Whilst opening up and letting it out
Did not make it go away
The disturbance it was causing
Meant it simply could not stay

So she did as she was guided
And took that leap of faith
She studied and she listened
In the therapist she did swathe

There clearly would be a change
Although it wouldn't be overnight
But knowing her true purpose
She would focus on her light

For she was a force to be reckoned with
When you truly knew her well
But could she get the old her back?
Only time could tell.

Knife Test

Oscillating, pumpernickel, serendipity, silhouette

The words that sound so beautiful, wind up like a cassette

Pronunciation, syllables, all wrapped around the tongue

Speaking, writing, expressing words, talking even sung

Communication connects us, different variations of speech

Understanding, comprehension which educators teach

The beauty of words never fails, with clear fascination

Writing letters, reading words, and reviewing a situation

We must retain the passion for words, essential and idyllic

Without them blandness certain, a world that's non specific

So use your words to talk, to challenge, read, shout and write

And allow the English language, always to excite!

Sponge

Satisfaction guaranteed, a false smile plastered on
Never knowing what is real, or seeing right from
wrong

Each day we update a status, always wanting a
reaction
Scrolling mindlessly through photographs, a constant
negative distraction

The lack of authenticity, and looking for realisation
Of the need for people to thumbs up, the constant
validation

We would rather record a life event than see it
through our own eyes
Updating followers as priority when a family member
dies

We've lost the heart in all we do when a number we
become
A slave to a screen we seem to be, when to social
media we succumb.

Flour

Her sparkles gained attention
Eyes shining so bright
Her aura glowed a soft pale yellow
Resembling a home warm light

Her smile made others feel welcome
Her dimples gleaming through
Her golden hair swayed gently
Against her eyes of deep sea blue

But behind the anesthetics
Her heart would often ache
For being seen as 'pretty'
Was not all that she could make

They failed to see the beauty
Of her kindness locked within
And how the tabs insider her brain
Often left her in a spin

As although her outside features
Were paramount to most
He recognised her heart warmth
Her personality he would boast

For in his recognition
Of the way she lived her life
Came the indication that she
Would one day be his wife

So despite the dimples, sea blue eyes
And golden hair which swayed
She began to love him deeply
In her heart is where he stayed.

Sugar

Rough around the edges
The darkest shade of brown
Her golden tresses bunched upon
The summit like a crown
Despite the scruffy appearance
Its aroma felt like home
Pulled from the metal grid
Butter gliding over the dome
Upon a plate or solitary
The softness of the sponge
The first slice for the favourite child
The one to take the plunge
The drizzle sparked the satisfaction
From both mouth and tum
Mouths full with baked goodness
The only eligible word was 'yum!'

Eggs

A brand new beginning
A plain white fresh clean page
A wonderous start again she saw
With vast opportunities to gage

Not often does this happen -
A chance to start again
Wonderful new encounters to build
A fresh connection chain

The excitement felt so transparent
A shared renewed bloom
An understanding of past failures noted
A space for new made room.

Burn

Flickering so gently, but with purpose nonetheless

Wick turned black with orange flame, the wax tries to confess

As it fills the jar, aroma spreading through the air

Curled up warm and cosy, observation within her stare

A hint of vanilla met with accompanying pumpkin spice

The dancing image within the flames attempting to entice

A single blow means disappearing and smoke climbs to the ceiling

Amazing how a simple candle can provide one so much healing

Butter

Scrolling through her messages, patience wearing thin

Waiting for the confirmation, scratching at her chin

Minutes felt like hours, waiting hurt her soul

She felt as though the current time, had fallen in a hole

Anticipation brewing, a yes, a no, or maybe...

Just waiting for the news to come felt like expecting a baby

But this wasn't a birth announcement she was waiting for

Unfortunately the 'yes' would make her fall upon the floor

A howl through pain of sincere loss where the tears were coming from

When it was confirmed by all - her dearest friend was gone.

Drizzle

Looking out of the window, wind blowing fast
Flowers and trees drinking moisture whilst it lasts

Raindrops falling heavily, reflections now distorted
Daydreaming for sunny climates, a wish to be
transported

Although there's something quite relaxing about these
rainy days
Cuddled up in blankets, looking through the haze

Remembering the last time we felt so intimate and
warm
And the irony of serendipity, caused by an external
storm

For within the clouds and rain, a clearing seems to
come
To open up the possibility of some much needed
warm sun

Refreshed and cleansed we often feel when the storm
has gone away
And within the blankets, daydreaming, is where we
choose to stay.

Spoon

We often take for granted, the smaller things in life
Complaining of the darkness, the pain, the loss, the strife
The days pass by, the sun goes down, the snow, the wind, the rain
But during all the heartache, the world remains the same.
Events and daily tasks unchanged, the clock continues to tick
The days merge into weeks then months, all moving so quick
So recognise the sunlight, the moments when we smile
For time is short for all of us, only present for a while.

Crisp

Vocabulary escaped her
Here comes the creative block
Then suddenly the words come flooding
Striking akin an electric shock

Never could she understand
The difference between the hours
One minute a complete emptiness
Followed by confidence blooming like flowers.

Timing

Childhood a battleground
Teen years also bleak
Young adults are conditioned
And encouraged not to speak

The system tries to shape us
An almost war like technique
Never making distant plans
Or allowed to reach our peak

Its time to rebel against it
And challenge all the rules
Pushing against the judgement
The control that begins in schools

They argue our 'best interests'
But really they want control
They wont be truly happy
Until our freedom they have stole

So stand up and speak your truth
Even if others don't agree
I'm asking will you challenge them
And stand strong with me?

Serve

Jupiter, Pluto, Saturn, Mars
She wished so often up to the stars
The galaxies, meteors and black holes
Endless atoms with different roles
Although so dark and hard to reach
Space and planets she would self teach
For there's something exciting about what we cant see
The mindful option to just 'be.'
Interstellar gases and birth charts galore
Learning the moon phases and so much more
Just the understanding that there is more to life than Earth
Our lives already decided, straight from individual birth.

The Cooling Tin

Amidst the darkness
She shone her light
Akin to a lighthouse
So unique and bright
Magnifying the spaces
Of safeness and home
Allowing the observer
To feel less alone.
The stability and protection
When the journey felt a blur
But the point remained so clearly...
Who was there for her?

Bitter

Growth through change and circumstance

We would often question why

Mistakes we make are troublesome

If no lessons learned or try -

To understand the reasons why we repeat the
same old thing

Or see our battles as mysterious

And races we must win

Not realising the expansions we make

As individual beings

When we come to realise the benefits

Of our mental freeing

So when we feel that all is lost

And companionship we seek

Growth through change and circumstance

Is the ultimate technique.

Tea

Milky, black, one lump or two
Earl Grey, blackcurrant, something new
Upon a plate stirred round and round
Spoon making that familiar clinking sound
Hand grasped tight around the mug
The first sip feeling like a welcome hug
Nostalgic and like home to me
Nothing beats a cup of tea!

Sweet

Symmetrical and delicate, it lands upon a leaf
A previous role within a cocoon not knowing what's beneath

Once embedded on the ground, looking up to the sky
Dreaming of the future and the ability to fly

When time came to sacrifice the life that it once knew
Wrapping itself up tightly, knowing that sleep was when it grew -

It's wings that it had longed for, pushed out of the self nest
Unique places to explore and conquer, a terrifying quest

Life now seemed more pleasant, as people watched it go by
Admiring the intense symmetrical beauty, of the graceful butterfly.

Little Lemon

A warm August evening, he came into the light
Weighing 6lb 3 ounces, he cried with all his might
Big purple alien eyes, soon to turn bright blue
Silky blonde head of hair, the smell that made him new.
His mottled skin and tiny nails, his hand picked babygrow
Looking back at photos - feeling like a lifetime ago.
Now nearly a decade, of seeing him grow into his skin
His laugh, his personality, the tiny man within
He likes the sameness and routine, of knowing what is next
His special brain I have had to learn is really quite complex
And no matter what he grows to be, I will support him out loud
And hope he knows that everyday, I am extremely proud.

9 789357 441575